OUR UNCONDITIONAL WALTZ

MY LIFE IN POEMS

NICOLETTA M. COSENTINO

Text Copyright © 2021 Nicoletta M. Cosentino
Published by Open Kimono Publishing, LLC
All rights reserved.
ISBN: 9798745572562
Hardcover ISBN:978-1-7377362-6-4

Dedication

To my family- my parents, husband, children, grandchildren and sister, I love you all very much. Family is everything, thank you God for blessing us with each other. Also to all my doggies; you're the embodiment of innocence and happiness- you have brought us all so much joy! As a former veterinarian technician and avid animal lover I am inclined by decree of their paws to include that ha!

THE LITTLE MIRACLE OF AUNTIE HELEN -1996

I open my eyes wider, staring in disbelief at what I am seeing, trying to take in more of what it is so that I can make sense of the shimmering, glistening, movement of colorful light in front of me. I sit up and reach my hand through it to feel if it is real. My hand goes directly through it, cutting into the movement of it's bright aura while it just silently remains there. I am in awe of the beauty- her beauty. I suddenly know that it is her- my favorite Great Aunt; I *feel* her presence. Her love, her essence, her very soul; there is no doubt in my mind *it is her* that I am looking at- even though the shimmering light does not resemble a person. My eyes catch the dimly lit red numbers displayed on my clock, it is three twenty-three in the morning. I turn back to the light but she is gone. She gradually fades away, making my bedroom wardrobe clearly in view, there's no longer a haze lingering between us. I am overcome with an immense happiness in that I knew she felt happy, content, and safe. I drifted back to sleep without even thinking about what it all meant. The heat of sun peaking through my window slowly awakens me; the high pitch ringing of my phone peels open my eyes.

I answer the call to realize that it's my momma on the other end of the line. I immediately pick up on the sheer hesitation in her voice and I know something is wrong.

Crying, she says, "Auntie Helen passed away.".

Instantly, my heart breaks; but I regain clarity of what woke me last night- the unmistakable feelings of contentment, safety and happiness flow back through me. I believe Auntie Helen appeared to me to tell me goodbye for now, but not forever, and that she was okay- better then okay. She knew we would all have such a hard time with her passing so she was leaving me with this one last gift. I was astonished at what I had experienced and so very thankful she had shared this with me.

When all of our family met at her house before her funeral, the clocks were all stopped at exactly three twenty-three in the morning. I inquired about this and was told that was the time Auntie Helen had passed away. It was the same time I had looked at the clock when she appeared to me in all her sparkling glory.

NICOLETTA M. COSENTINO

LOST - 1988

A Puzzle That Cannot
    Be put together
The pieces have
Vanished - I go on
Unwillingly
Trying
To forget
The bad parts,
The sad parts
Which wont
Go Away.
The best parts
Have been
Misplaced…
Lost.

ONE FISH - 1989

One
      Solitary fish
Deserted from all
Yet fearful
To stand tall.
The entire ocean
Is full of interest
Filled with discoveries
Waiting to be made
But
One fish
Is afraid-
To discover
To seek
To find the unwanted.

Saltwater can sting
Enough to make fish shout,
But tides, great waters, and waves
Wash the sting out.
Drowning in a sea
Of uncertainty
Beginning to feel ill,
Swimming alone
Treading water
All at a muffled
Standstill.
Cruelness
And harshness
Cause
Curiosity
To be stifled,
Who can be
Trusted
Without two rifles?
To make his world
A friendly place
One fish
Must have a
Magic potion,
How can one fish- Be a fish
Without exploring the ocean?

HALLOWEEN - 1989

Candles burning
    Shadows playing on the wall
Creatures lurking around the corner
No one knows
Where
They will fall.
Witches will
Cackle cruelly
Wind will
Scream and howl
Bats will
Fly furiously
The word
HALLOWEEN
Has casted a spell.

OUR UNCONDITIONAL WALTZ

There's no way out
Trapped forever
HALLOWEEN
Is a game
Played only
By the Clever.

SOMETIMES - 1989

Sometimes you didn't understand.
    And it made me cry.
Sometimes you wouldn't lend
Me a hand, and I thought I would die.
Sometimes I couldn't stand on my own,
But maybe you were right behind me -
We came so far in life
And I finally could find me
No sooner than when I knew
Myself so very well,
And I end up just like water
Without a well.
    Where am I headed? I ask. Sometimes, I can't tell.

BROKEN GLASSES - 1987

Piercing
　　　Shatter of Glass -
Bent, broken metal frames
Crushed
In the rocks, or against wooden paneling
Rush to pick up the pieces,
To cling to safety behind a locked
Bathroom door
How I hated those angry moments,
Harsh words, and screaming voices.
Next....
The slamming of the front door.
Heavy footsteps stomping to the truck
Light footsteps chasing, pleading,
An angry engine Growls.

NICOLETTA M. COSENTINO

    Scared, Unhappy Crying
Continues through the night.
It's a Hellish nightmare
But when morning arrives,
It was just another Fight.
Swollen knuckles and holes in the wall.
May recover, The dark attic in my mind
May Not.

SILENCE - 1988

Silence
    Familiar sounds surround me
But there is always
Silence
As I watch the world
Around me
Stillness will continue
To have found me
Silence
My heart searches for
Happiness
My mind knows no
Peace
My eyes strain to look
For unknown sources

NICOLETTA M. COSENTINO

Of relief
Silence
I hear beyond the noises
Far past my 17 years
My youthful face
Won't show it
But my eyes reveal
The fear
Silence
I pretend to be young
But my silence slyly
Uncovers the truth
My childhood somehow
Escaped me
I fell far past
The age of youth
Silence
Voiceless words
Are heard
Without question
Soundless noises
Are amplified
In a sense
Still, here I stand in
Silence
My only, my best, Defense -SILENCE.

FAMILY SYMPHONY - 2021

God and I wrote a symphony together!
    There are three movements,
23 years later we added a
fourth made up of two Sonatas,

THIS SYMPHONY HAS GROWN with time
    It swells with love, change,
    And stanza after stanza of
    Beautiful harmonies.

OUR ARRANGEMENT IS in tune with
    The universe,

NICOLETTA M. COSENTINO

    The time signature a simple 3/4
    Giving the score a 1-2-3

1-2-3, 1-2-3,

WALTZING rhythm
    We choose to rely on
    All movements of the symphony
    To keep dancing.

OUR KEY SIGNATURE has
    Flats and sharps
    Because different
    Is wholeheartedly
    Accepted

WE ARE a Rhapsody of
    The chromatic scale
    Keeping middle C
    As our home base
    Branching off when needed
    But returning to the chorus

OUR UNCONDITIONAL WALTZ

By memory

Our symphony ends with
    A rollicking finale,
    Not meant to be the end
    But a beginning for
    Generations to come

THE COLOR OF BLACK - 1988

Black memories of **black** olives at Christmas dinner,
The shiny **black** lacquer of a grand piano, he sudden complete **blackness** of a power outage, **black** magic of witches in **black** robes,
A **black** widow creeping in a black corner, the deep black Forest smelling of burnt **black** wood, and **black** memories of
Night, with its rich, enveloping, darkness of **black**.

WHERE - 1987

Where
    Can I find pure happiness?
I'm willing to look
Through dark forests and crowded streets.
Where-
Ever my instincts lead me,
I will follow
With anxious eyes
And weary feet.
Where
Will I find true happiness?
The search may
Never end-
Only

NICOLETTA M. COSENTINO

Every time I'm with you
Enough happiness I have to lend!
Where
Have I found true happiness?
It is in your touch,
Your eyes, Your kiss-Where
Is true, pure happiness?
I need not look
Farther than this.

RAZZLE DAZZLE - 1989

Running
    Away
Zipping and
Zooming
Like a never-
Ending lightning bolt
Daring
Anyone to
Zip and
Zoom after him
Like an
Eagle flying dog

MOM, THE KING OF ROCK AND ROLL, AND I - 1992

Like The King of Rock and Roll said…..
    Memories-
You were there for me
Creating
MEMORIES
That became my everyday life
And so
I remember to
Brush my teeth and say my prayers
Each night
To say please and thank you
Until it came naturally
And I
Watched

OUR UNCONDITIONAL WALTZ

You being thoughtful to others
You and your Mom
And I imitate you
All that time
You were watching me
Grow up safely
Become my own person
Believe in the values and morals
You gave me
And you
Remembered
To make me feel good about myself
To listen when I had something to say
And to LOVE me no matter what
Mom,
You gave me beautiful, important
Memories
For 21 years
And now with your help
I'd love to
Do the same for my baby
Like The King of Rock and Roll said
Memories…..

OUR SALVATION - 2021

When I close my eyes I'm there -
I feel
The glare-
But without their meandering stare
My senses fade to black, I'm instantly
Taken back
Before my heart could tear
Without vision or a care, all that's
Unfair fades,
Yet I'm relentlessly aware
Behind the curtains of my lashes lies an
Incomprehensible fare, served cold and old
Retold from our timeless story,
That fortune favors

OUR UNCONDITIONAL WALTZ

The brave - the bold
Sold lies from stolen life's- we live -
Some even grow old
The sun of today feels warmer
Even though it's cold
Or at least so I've been told
When I close my eyes I'm there- in a dark abyss
All is fair

GRANDPA - 1986

GRANDPA
    This poem is for you, Grandpa
    For all the times
you came creaking
Down the stairs
With a juicy watermelon
To make our childhood
summer days complete,
This is for the nickname you gave me
The day I was born- no one uses it now
I will always mourn its loss
And this is for your love
Of my unsure accordion playing
That catchy Italian Waltz
This is for your wish,

OUR UNCONDITIONAL WALTZ

Your wish to be there for graduation-
And my wedding-
You will be there Grandpa,
Because I carry you in my heart
This poem is for you, Grandpa
I know you will see it-
Even before it is carried to you
By a heaven bound bird.

FAMILY ON THE OTHER SIDE - 2000

We'll talk again in my dreams, after bedtime stories, lullabies. Together when I close my eyes. Sometimes a quiet moment, I'll seek you out, you are peaceful in your essence, I feel content with your familiar, treasured presence. Each surprise me in distinct ways, I sense your nearness through symbol- scent.

    We converse thoughts, and interpret thoughts you've lent. You keep away darkness, the shadows. I question my sanity explaining I **trust - believe** even if it leaves me floundering in awkward moments with those you wish you reached. Your sparkle and glisten of **life**, my heart won't leave. We'll talk again in my dreams, -surprise me, startle I will not.

My life isn't complete without all you've taught.

OUR WALTZ - 2000

*L*ife is a rhythmic dance where the world and all of it's inhabitants circle around in a never ending progression. The Earth will spin in perpetuity just as people will live their lives day in and day out- it's all so much like a waltz. What gives life meaning is relationships with one another, love, and the ability to enrich others lives by any means possible. At the end of the day, it boils down to an unconditional love that we can all show towards one another. Life is not perfect, neither is the world- and it never will be. Together though, we can embrace our unconditional waltz on this Earth hand in hand to be the best version of ourselves and prove that humanity can be a reflection of our best intentions. Idealism becomes realism when we choose love over hate- kindness over cruelty and exhibit true empathy for all. From the moment my children were born, I felt an unconditional, all encompassing love for them. They are the music in my soul. This is the seed for my below composition: *The Unconditional Waltz*; please feel free to play along!

THE UNCONDITIONAL WALTZ

OUR UNCONDITIONAL WALTZ

NICOLETTA M. COSENTINO

www.ingramcontent.com/pod-product-compliance
Lightning Source LLC
Chambersburg PA
CBHW021951160426
43209CB00030B/1907/J